OBJECT LESSONS
FROM
SCIENCE EXPERIMENTS

OBJECT LESSONS FROM SCIENCE EXPERIMENTS

RICHARD F. GEBHARDT
&
MARK ARMSTRONG

BAKER BOOK HOUSE
Grand Rapids, Michigan 49516

ISBN: 0-8010-3811-1

Fifth printing, July 1992

Printed in the United States of America

Richard F. Gebhardt, illustrator

Contents

Introduction

Communication in this age of high technology is still struggling for success. Humanity has made great advances over the past couple of centuries, although we continue to have problems. One of these problems originated with the beginning of civilization, yet we in this modern age tend to think we are too sophisticated to do what those beginners did to solve their "communication gap"—use visuals!

This book was developed to encourage better communication through the use of visual examples, also called *experiments*. We have incorporated interesting examples within the lessons to help you reach more young people. After all, in many situations in the Bible, examples were used to stress ideas. In Exodus 7:8–10, for instance, the Lord changed a rod into a serpent for Moses and Aaron to prove a point to the Pharaoh. Jesus also used many examples that his followers could easily relate to. In Matthew 13 is the parable of the sower as well as an explanation of why Jesus used parables. Jesus gave illustrations so that his audience could easily follow his points.

Using examples in your lessons by offering object lessons will make your lessons more meaningful, stimulate more interest, and encourage retention of the subject matter. You will also find that these experiments will prove interesting to adults as well as to youth. The lessons are relatively short so they may be used as junior sermons or for church school opening exercises. The lessons should work well for youth group meetings and may be appealing enough to feature as a theme for a quarter.

The format of each lesson should be easy to work with. The lesson Theme and Illustration appear at the beginning for easy reference.

The Lesson itself is in a conversational tone and provides the complete story line, with clearly marked inserted instructions where you are to perform some part of the experiment.

How It Works goes into the experiment in detail so you can set it up and present it successfully. An illustration is included to aid in better understanding of the setup arrangements.

A Principle section is added to many of the lessons to explain further why the experiment reacted as it did.

Finally, an AV Options section to some of the lessons introduces other ways of presenting the experiment, primarily to help your audience see or understand what is being done. Sometimes you will have to explain what is happening because part of the audience may not be able to see the phenomenon that is occurring.

Remember that Practice is necessary for success. Take

time at home to go completely through each experiment. You will do a much better job if you do not have to worry about the success of the experiment while you speak and interact with your audience. Know where you have to place the various elements of the experiment. Be sure that you have readied certain parts and potions before the presentation to save time.

Leave as little as possible to chance. *Never* modify an experiment at the time of presentation from the way you practiced it, or you may discover that the experiment does not work the same. You could be embarrassed; the audience will lose the point of the lesson, and the impact of the lesson will be diminished.

1

Solving Our Problems

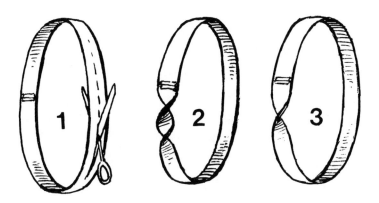

Theme

There are three ways of solving your problems: by your-self, with the help of others, and with God. The results of each may be quite different.

Illustration

Three large paper loops, when cut down the middle, will produce three different results.

Materials

three loops of adding machine paper
scissors
scotch tape

How It Works

Each of the paper loops is made of 5 or 6 feet of adding machine paper or any kind of paper cut to about 1 inch wide. The ends of Loop 1 are to be connected with scotch tape to form a continuous loop without any twists. Loop 2 will be connected after twisting one end 360 degrees around (a complete turn). Loop 3 will be connected after twisting one end only 180 degrees around (a half turn).

When Loop 1 is cut along the middle all the way around the loop, it will come apart into two separate loops. Loop 2 will become two separate loops linked together. Loop 3 will become one large circle. Ask the helpers to hold their loops up for the audience to see when they finish cutting.

Lesson

(Choose three volunteers. Give a paper loop to each one and ask them to cut down the middle around the loops at the proper time.)

Often when we have a decision to make or we are facing a problem, we try to solve it alone or we look for someone to answer our questions or suggest solutions. We become so caught up with our problems that we don't stop to pray for God's answers. Because of that, the solution may look completely different from what it really should be. In reality, when we ask for God's direction, we become tuned to his thinking and are on the right track to the solution.

(Ask a helper to cut loop 1.)

Many times we think we can solve our own problems without the help of anyone else, even God. Sometimes when we try to solve a problem ourselves, we only make matters worse. Instead of having one problem to take care of, we have two. This complication is definitely not what God wants for our lives.

(The first loop, when cut, will become two separate loops. Ask another helper to cut down the middle of loop 2.)

Sometimes we think that we need someone else to help us. By talking to our friends, we may decide on a good solution but it is possible that the solution may not totally match God's desires.

(The second cut loop will become two loops intertwined with each other. Ask the other helper to cut around loop 3.)

When we go to God, we can become completely in accord with his will, and our solution will be the same as his. In Proverbs 3:5–6 we read, "Trust in the Lord with all your heart, and do not lean on your own understanding. In all your ways acknowledge Him, and He will make your path straight" (NASB). When we have problems, we need to go to God for answers, and he will guide us.

(The third cut loop comes out as one continuous loop.)

In the Bible James (1:5) says, "If any of you lacks wisdom, he should ask God, . . . and it will be given to

15

him" (NIV). He means that when we need to find an answer to a problem, we can and should go to God so he will guide us toward what he wants us to do. By doing so we will know his will.

2

How God Provides Salvation

COIN IS LEFT HIGH AND DRY

WATER COVERS THE COIN

Theme

Because God is perfect, he can not allow sin in heaven. Therefore, because we are sinful, he has to remove our sins in order to allow us in heaven.

Illustration

A dime covered with water on a saucer can be retrieved without anyone's fingers ever getting wet.

Materials

saucer water
matches a dime
short candle a glass

How It Works

Before the lesson, drip some wax onto the center of the saucer and stand the short candle upright. The glass must be tall enough to avoid touching the flame when it is inverted and placed over the candle. The water will be drawn up into the glass when the flame goes out. The coin will be left exposed.

Principle

The flame on the candle burns all of the oxygen within the glass when it is placed over the candle in the water, leaving a vacuum in the glass and less pressure inside than outside. Nature tries to equalize conditions whenever possible, so the water is drawn inside to equalize pressures.

Lesson

The Bible describes heaven, the most beautiful place that we could ever imagine. In heaven there are gates of pearl, streets made of pure gold, and every precious gem imaginable, including diamonds and rubies. Heaven is such a beautiful place that God wants everyone to go there. God is there and he allows no sin in heaven. But the problem is, we have sin in our lives.

The apostle Paul writes in Romans 3:23 that "all have sinned and fall short of the glory of God" (NASB). Every human who has ever lived has been sinful, but God, who is perfect, cannot allow sin to enter heaven. Therefore, sin stops us from going to heaven.

But, God loves us so much that he still wants us to come to heaven. So he made a way to remove our sin so we can go to heaven. John (3:16) says, "For God so loved the world that He gave His only begotten son, that whoever believes in Him should not perish, but have eternal life" (NASB). God loves you and me so much that he sent Jesus down to earth to die on a cross for us. He died, not for any wrong he had done (because he was perfect), but to take care of our sin so we could be with God in heaven when we die. All we have to do is believe this fact and personally accept him as our Savior. Our sin will then be removed so we will be able to go to heaven when the time comes.

To show what these verses mean we will let this saucer represent the earth, and this coin will represent a person living on the earth.

(Place the coin in the saucer toward the edge. Pour some water into the saucer so that the coin is covered. A helper might be asked if the coin can be lifted out without getting wet fingers.)

The water will represent sin. There is no way to get the coin off the saucer without getting wet, and we surely don't want to put our fingers in sin. Likewise, there is no way for God to get us to heaven without doing something about that sin.

(Light the candle and place the inverted glass over it. Most of the water will be drawn up into the glass and the coin will be out of the water.)

Now let's remove that sin. The glass represents God's cover of our sin. The flame is Jesus, who died for our sins. As he died, our sins were removed.

(Now ask your helper to tell the audience if the coin can be taken without getting in hot water.)

Just as this glass and candle removed the water from the coin, Jesus removed our sins when he died on the cross.

Now let me ask, how do you get that coin? To get that coin you have to reach out and take it. This is the same thing we must do to be able to go to heaven. Even though Jesus died for our sin, we must reach out through prayer and personally accept him as Savior.

3

God Knows Our Thoughts

Theme

God always knows what we are thinking, and we need to make sure that our thoughts are pleasing to him.

Illustration

Write something on a piece of glass with your finger. No one can read it until you breathe onto the glass, making the words become visible.

Materials

a clean pane of glass
a glass of soapy water

How It Works

Dip your finger into a glass of soapy water and write something on a clean glass with the wet finger. Be sure that the pane of glass is thoroughly washed and free from any skin oils or soap. The wet image will soon dry and become invisible to the eye. When you breathe on the pane of glass, the soapy image will not cloud with vapors.

Principle

The soapy solution leaves a filmy layer on the otherwise clean pane of glass. The soapy image will not cloud as you breathe on it. Oily fingerprints also will not cloud, so be careful how you handle the glass.

AV Option

Show the audience that the glass looks blank by using the overhead projector; when you breathe on the message, it will project.

Lesson

Some people in this world claim to be mind readers. Actually, there is no such thing as a mind reader. Often they have been informed ahead of time of the things a person plans to say. Can anyone here tell me what I am thinking right now?

(Dip your finger into the solution and write a message on the glass.)

Our mind is like this piece of glass. If I use my finger to write something on it you probably won't be able to see what I have written. Like the message on this glass, you can not read what's in my mind. No human on this earth can actually read someone else's mind. There is one, however, who always knows what's in our minds and what we are thinking. That one is God. No matter how hard we try to keep him from knowing what we are thinking, we can't prevent it. Even though we can't read each other's minds, God can. Nothing can be hidden from him.

(Breathe hard on the message area of the glass, causing moisture to form over the entire message. Hold it up for the audience to see.)

When I breathe on this glass, you can see what I have written on it. To God, it is as if I have written my thoughts on a piece of paper. In Job 21:27 God says, "Behold, I know your thoughts, and the plans by which you would wrong me" (NASB). At home, at school, or wherever we are, we need to remember that God knows what we are thinking, and what we think should be pleasing to him. As the rest of that verse suggests, we must not hurt him with mean or bad thoughts.

4

Letting Our Light Shine

Theme

If you want to tell your friends about Jesus, your life must first reflect the light of Jesus.

Illustration

Placing a small mirror at an angle in a bowl of water and shining a light through it will cause an array of colors to bounce onto the ceiling.

Materials

three bowls   a flashlight
two pocket mirrors   water in two of the bowls

How It Works

Place three bowls on the table, with a pocket mirror in the second and third bowls, resting at an angle of about 30 degrees to the surface of the table. Fill the first and third bowls about ¾ full of water, and leave the second bowl empty. Darken the room.

When you shine the flashlight into the mirror in the water, you should see a rainbow of colors reflecting on the ceiling. When you shine the light into the bowl with water in it, you might see waves on the ceiling, and when the light is shined into the bowl with a mirror and no water, you should see a plain light reflected on the ceiling.

Principle

Isaac Newton proved that light is made up of rays of different wave lengths. His most famous experiment used a prism and a beam of sunlight. The water acts as a prism, separating the wave lengths to be seen as different colors.

AV Options

Practice beforehand so you know at what angle to hold the light. Keep in mind what the ceiling is like in the room you will ultimately be using.

Lesson

Jesus wants us to tell our friends about him and how to become a Christian. Sometimes, though, it is hard to tell them about Jesus because they will not listen to us. There might be a reason why they don't listen to us. Let me illustrate why.

(Turn the flashlight on. Shine it at the audience, then into bowl 1, which has no mirror in the water.)

Some of us show that God is in our lives in only small ways. Let's say that this light represents God's influence. His light is shining on us and we will reflect his light through our lifestyles. But notice on the ceiling that this person appears to reflect very little of God in his or her lifestyle.

(Point the flashlight into bowl 2, containing a mirror and no water.)

Some of us might be devoted followers of Jesus yet do not let our strong belief show to others. As you can see from God's light, this person reflects a lot of God's influence. However, this reflection is very plain, not very colorful, telling us that this person does the right things in life but may not do them to honor the Lord. In other words, here is a Christian who doesn't glow with the joy of knowing Jesus. There may be an attitude missing, a pleasant and joyful attitude.

(Point the flashlight into bowl 3, with a mirror and water in it.)

In Matthew 5:16 Jesus tells us that there is a better way to witness to others. He says, "Let your light so shine before men that they may see your good works, and glorify your Father which is in heaven" (KJV). He means that our friends should be able to tell that we are Christians by our actions, and that they should notice that there is something different about the way we live. It might be that we don't get mad as others do and that we don't swear or say some of the things that others do. We should have a happiness in the things we do that shows that we like being Christians. This happiness suggests that we have God in our hearts. Our actions should invite others to want to share the same kind of joy that we have. Our true colors should show, just as the true colors of this light show on the ceiling to all of us. If your life reflects God's blessings, it will be easy to tell others because they will know that you mean what you say because you live the way you do.

5

A Little Sin Goes a Long Way

Theme

How much effect does a little sin have? Only a little sin can cloud a whole life.

Illustration

A glass of clear water, slowly colored by adding iodine, finally becomes dark, but can be cleared again.

Materials

a clear drinking glass water
iodine some used hypo-fixative
an eye dropper

How It Works

Regular iodine from the drug store is strong in color and can be dropped into water in very small amounts to show much coloration. A couple of drops with an eye dropper will work each time.

Hypo-fixative is one of the most common chemicals used by photographers for fixing their photos in the development process. We suggest that you ask for a small amount from any friend who does picture printing. A cupful will be more than you need. Used hypo works well for this process. New hypo can also be purchased at a photo store or at any drug store that sells photo supplies.

Principle

The hypo-fixative chemically neutralizes the iodine. With such small amounts of iodine in the water, you should be able to neutralize your glassful easily.

Lesson

The exciting thing about being a Christian is that we can have a life that is crystal clear and clean, just like this water. We read in 1 John 1:9 that if we confess our sin to God, he is faithful to take away all of our sin and to make us clean from all our unrighteousness. So when we do sin, we can tell God what we have done, and he will remove our sins from us and make us clean again, just like this glass of water.

Sometimes, though, we get a little careless and think that just a small amount of sin isn't so bad. Let this iodine represent sin, and we will see what just a little sin can do to the clean water that represents our clean image.

(Pour a few drops of iodine into the water.)

When we do things that aren't right, that is sin. For example, imagine you are downtown with your friends and they are all buying candy bars. Let's suppose that you don't have any money with you and you want a candy bar. It would seem simple to grab one and put it in your pocket when no one is looking and walk out of the store without paying for it. You might even think that you'll come back and pay for it sometime. You may think that this is just a little sin, and that it doesn't make very much difference because it didn't cost very much.

(Drop a little more iodine into the glass.)

Maybe the next day you go to school and the teacher gives a quiz that you forgot to study for, so you decide to look at someone else's paper. You think that this too is just a little sin and that you don't need to confess it.

(Drop more iodine into the glass.)

Then when you get home after playing with your friends, your mother says not to eat anything before dinner, but those cookies sure smell good! Anyway, she'll never notice that only one is missing. When she asks if you ate anything, you say no. You figure that it is just a little lie, and that it is no big deal.

(Drop more iodine into the glass.)

You may think that each of these sins is just a little thing and doesn't affect you, but that is not true. The apostle Paul tells us in 1 Corinthians 5:6, "Do you not know that a little leaven leavens the whole lump of dough?" (NASB). Now leaven is yeast, and when a baker or your mom makes bread, she puts a little leaven in the dough and mixes it until all of the dough has leaven in it. It takes only a little leaven to cause the whole amount of dough to rise.

It works the same as this iodine. We added only a little at a time, but you can see how dark the water looks now. This is also true of our sin. We may think that a little sin each day doesn't make much difference, but it really does. What you and I have to do is confess our sin to God, and when we do, he will forgive us, simply because he promised to. We shouldn't wait until we have sinned a lot before we confess, but should do it each time we sin so we can stay clean.

(Pour some hypo-fixative into the solution.)

Your sins will be cleared as nicely as this water if you handle those little sins properly. However, you do not have the privilege of sinning as often as you want just because you know that God will forgive you each time. If you think this way, then you are not earnest in your request for forgiveness as you confess. Insincerity doesn't work when we talk to God about our sins.

6

How to Understand the Bible

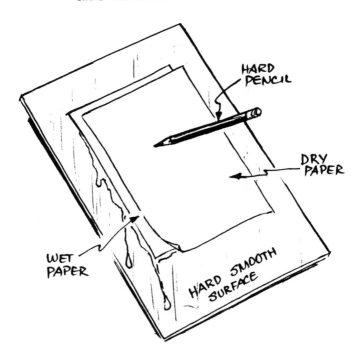

HARD PENCIL

DRY PAPER

WET PAPER

HARD SMOOTH SURFACE

Theme

Because the Holy Spirit wrote the Bible, the only way we can understand it fully is to have him guide our minds as we read it.

Illustration

A blank piece of paper will show a message after it has been soaked in water.

Materials

two pieces of paper	paper towels
a pan of water	plate glass/mirror
hard lead pencil or ball-point pen	

How It Works

Soak a piece of paper in water, then place it onto a smooth, hard surface, such as a piece of glass, a mirror, or a formica counter top. Cover the wet paper with a dry piece of paper and proceed to write your message with the pencil or ball-point pen. Take the dry piece off and you should easily see the message imprinted on the wet paper. Put the wet paper on a paper towel to help it dry. When dry, you should not be able to see the message at all, but it will appear again when the paper is placed in water.

AV Options

If you hold the paper in front of a light for the audience, the water mark will be evident, even though it may be difficult to read from a distance.

Lesson

If you want to understand the meaning of something in a book, the author is the best person to explain it for you.

This principle is also true of the Bible. In 2 Peter 1:20–21 we read that "no prophecy of the Scripture is of any private interpretation. For the prophecy came not in old time by the will of man: but holy men of God spake as they were moved by the Holy Ghost" (KJV). Here, we are told that the Holy Spirit was guiding the men who wrote the Scriptures and told them what to write. So we know that the Holy Spirit is the author of the Bible.

In order to understand the Bible, we need to ask the Holy Spirit to help us see what was meant when it was written. Even scholars have had difficulty in determining some interpretations. We are not able to grasp all of what the Bible actually means unless we have help, and the Holy Spirit is the best helper.

(Ask someone to come up.)

A message is on this piece of paper. Would you please read it for us?

(Wait for helper to try.)

You are perfectly right when you say that the message can't be read because it is hard to see. Sometimes the Bible's message is hard to see, too. We are not going to be able to get the true message by ourselves every time we look into our Bibles.

Would you like to have me help you find out what the message really is on that piece of paper? I can tell you how to bring the hidden message out clearly—would you like me to?

(Tell the helper to dip the paper into the water.)

The water is like the Holy Spirit. He helps us see what he wrote, and therefore we will have a better understanding. You may have some friends who say that they have tried reading the Bible but it doesn't make sense to them. That's because they can't understand it. The Holy Spirit may not be working in their lives to help them learn what it means. Once the Holy Spirit comes into our lives and we ask for his help, the Bible won't be as difficult to understand. It's much easier to read and understand once we trust him and communicate with him. Then we will begin to find more meaning and enjoyment from our reading of the Bible.

It is worth bringing out one more point here. I made my helper _____ go through the steps that you should go through to understand the Bible better. First, I let _____ know that I knew how to get the message out of the paper. We know that God knows what the Bible means. Then, I indicated that (s/he) could get help with the message if (s/he) wanted. We must ask God for his help also. Then I told (him/her) how to get the message. God is willing to help us understand what is written in the Bible if we ask for his help.

7

How God Sees Us

Theme

Even though we may sin, God sees us as though we have no sin.

Illustration

A postage stamp, when placed under a glass of water, is easily seen. But when a saucer is placed on the glass, the stamp seems to disappear.

Materials

a tall glass of water
a saucer
a postage stamp

How It Works

Place a postage stamp, face up, under a tall, clear glass that is about ¾ full of water. Looking down into the glass, you should be able to see the stamp easily. When a saucer is placed on top of the glass, however, it is impossible to see the stamp from any angle.

Principle

The light is being refracted at an angle through the water. Because of this angle, it is impossible to see the stamp when the glass is covered by a wider object.

AV Options

Because it is virtually impossible to project this phenomenon so that a group can see it, it is better to ask for an assistant, preferably a young person from the audience.

The two steps may be reversed for more of a surprise effect with some slight alteration to the story line, starting with the saucer on the glass and then removing it to reveal a clever saying or drawing under the glass.

Lesson

When God looks at his followers, what does he see? Does he see any sin? God knows that we sin. However, he looks on us as though we have no sin because of what Christ did for us on the cross.

(Ask a helper to look down into the glass and describe what can be seen.)

Before a person accepts Jesus as Savior, his or her sins are easily seen by God. As he looks at us, he sees the wrongs that separate us from him. God wants us to have part in his kingdom, but until we accept Jesus and confess the wrong things we have done, we are prevented from having a relationship with God. That is when he can see the sins that we continue to have.

(Cover the glass with a saucer and ask your helper to tell what can be seen.)

When we receive Christ as Savior, God does not see our sins because Christ has paid the penalty and covered our sins. Just as we read in Psalm 103:12, "As far as the east is from the west, so far has He removed our transgressions from us" (NASB). When we become Christians, God removes our sins far away. You and I will never stop sinning, and God knows that. But if we confess our sins, God no longer sees them, but sees us as if we had not sinned at all.

8

Helping Friends Who Have a Conflict

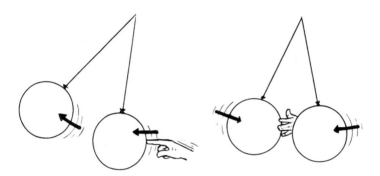

Theme

When two of our friends are having a conflict, we should try to help them resolve their problem.

Illustration

Two balloons, tied to separate strings, stay apart even when one is pushed toward the other. However, if you put your hand between them, they are drawn together to your hand.

Materials

two inflated balloons on long strings
a piece of wool

How It Works

After inflating the two balloons, tie them to two long pieces of string and tie the string ends together. Rub the balloons with the piece of wool to build a charge of static electricity. Some furs and other kinds of cloth may work as well, or you could even try rubbing them on your hair. Hold the ends of the strings so the ballons will hang down equally or hang the strings over the end of a yardstick projecting out from something. Do not let them rest against the wall. This will cause them to lose their charge. The balloons will visibly repel each other, even when you push one toward the other. When you bring your hand between the balloons, they will be attracted to your hand.

Principle

The identical ions in the balloons repel each other. The reverse is true when your hand is placed between them; the opposite ions in your hand attract those in the balloons.

Lesson

All of us have friends who sometimes don't get along. Perhaps one said something that hurt the other's feelings, or they just don't agree on something. These two balloons can represent our two friends, rejecting each other and staying away from each other.

(Hold two balloons in one hand by their long strings.)

You might ask yourself if you should do anything about their problem. What does the Bible tell us to do in this situation? In Ephesians 4:3 we are told, "Make every effort to keep the unity of the Spirit through the bond of peace" (NIV). That is, we are supposed to help other people get along with each other when they have a problem. But sometimes we don't know how. We might go to one of them and try pushing them together. We suggest they become friends again, but they still stay apart.

(With your free hand push one balloon toward the other.)

Then, maybe we would encourage the other person. But that still might not work.

(Do the same with the other balloon.)

Paul tells us in Galatians 6:2 to "bear one another's burdens . . ." (NASB). In other words, we are to help them come together and work out their problem and to help each forgive the other person.

(Put your free hand between the two balloons. They will come together and cling to your hand.)

To do so we must be understanding and have patience. We must be cautious not to appear to be intruding into their business. Hopefully, you will help to bring them back together, and maybe closer to you, also.

9

God's Help in Our Lives

Theme

God is always available to help and protect us when we are in need. All we have to do is ask.

Illustration

A coin placed on a table next to a saucer will jump into the saucer when you blow across the top of the coin.

Materials

a regular saucer
a penny

How It Works

Place the saucer about 4 inches from the edge of the table. The coin should be placed about halfway between the edge of the table and the saucer. If you place your chin against the edge of the table and blow in a semi-strong puff across the top of the coin, the coin will lift up and fall into the saucer. "Semi-strong" means not as strong as you can but not too softly either. You should practice before showing the experiment so you can successfully instruct the volunteer or easily do it yourself. Make sure you blow across the coin, not at it.

AV Options

There are not many options for this experiment except to suggest that it be well lighted. A simple gooseneck table lamp shining down onto the coin and saucer should be helpful.

Lesson

(Prior to starting, get a volunteer. Place the saucer about 4 inches from the edge of the table. Put the coin in the saucer.)

This saucer represents the safety that God gives his children when troubles come. This coin represents you and me as Christians. As long as we are in God's care, we benefit from that care. When we step out of God's protection, trouble can possibly hurt us.

(As you talk, hold up the coin and then place it on the table halfway between the saucer and the table edge.)

When we realize that we have stepped out of God's protection, we need to ask him to bring us back into his care. James (4:2) tells us that we do not have because we do not ask. If we are out of God's protection, we won't have it unless we ask for it. But, as soon as we ask, God has promised he will help us and give us the strength we need to get back into his protective care.

(Ask your helper if the coin can be put into the saucer without touching it.)

Yes, it can, with the help of air. Does this sound impossible?

(Ask the volunteer to place his or her chin against the table and blow over the coin in a short puff. The coin should hop into the saucer.)

In Jeremiah 33:3 the Lord says, "Call unto me, and I will answer thee, and show thee great and mighty things, which thou knowest not" (KJV). God promises to come and help us and put us back into his protection if we ask. Also, he may put us back in an unusual way. It is possible to do the seemingly impossible with God's help. We can't always see his help, but it's there.

10

Living by Faith

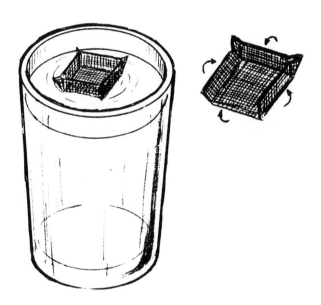

Theme

As Christians, we are told to live by faith. Faith is believing that what God tells us in the Bible is true.

Illustration

A boat made from a wire screen can float on water even though it has many holes in it.

Materials

a tall transparent glass
a small piece of window screen

How It Works

Cut a small piece of metal window screen and bend the sides up to form a small boat (see diagram). Fill the glass about ⅔ full of water so the audience can look through the glass and see the boat on top of the water.

Place the screen flat on the surface of the water. It will float indefinitely.

Principle

Water that is untainted with a foreign substance, such as soap, has a natural surface tension. The molecules are attracted to each other, creating a cohesion, clinging together. This works across the top of the water from one side of the glass to the other, as it does between every wire of the mesh boat, providing enough surface tension to prevent the boat from breaking through the surface.

AV Options

This experiment is very difficult to enlarge but can be dramatized by placing a spotlight so the shadow shows on a bare wall or a projection screen. The light will help the audience to more easily see the boat on the water. It would help to have an assistant (preferably a youth from the audience) describe for the audience what is seen as the experiment progresses.

Lesson

In Romans 1:17 we read, "the righteousness of God is revealed from faith to faith; as it is written, 'but the righteous man shall live by faith'" (NASB). In order to please God and do what is right, we Christians are to live by faith. What is faith? Faith is having firm and earnest belief in the statements of another person that something is true even though we haven't seen it.

If I tell you that I can make a piece of metal float on water, you'll probably say it's impossible. But if I also tell you that the metal is shaped like a boat, then you'll probably agree that it will float. Well, I have made a little boat from a piece of metal. But, look at all the holes in it. What happens to a boat with a hole in it? It sinks! Look at this boat. Do you think it will float or sink? How many of you think this boat will float when I put it in this glass of water?

(Very few, if any, hands may be raised.)

Now, if I tell you that I *know* this boat will float when I put it on the water, how many of you believe what I say?

(More hands may go up.)

If you believe me, then you have faith. You believe that what I said is true, even though you haven't seen it.

(Put the screen boat on the water. Let everyone see that it floats.)

See, you were right to have faith in me because what I said was true. Not everything I say is always right; sometimes I make mistakes. But does God ever make mistakes? No! Can we always have faith in him that everything he says is true? Yes!

(**End by sharing some of the things God has said that we can believe and have faith in, e.g., John 3:16, Ephesians 6:1–2, 1 John 1:9, and Hebrews 13:5b.**)

11

Enduring Under Pressure

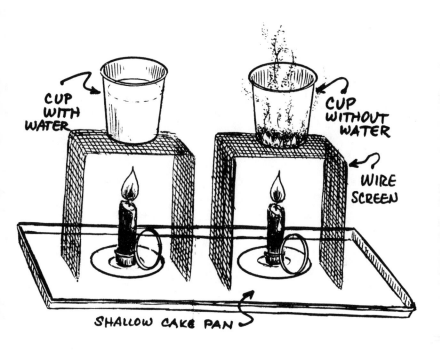

CUP WITH WATER

CUP WITHOUT WATER

WIRE SCREEN

SHALLOW CAKE PAN

Theme

Everyone reacts differently under pressure from others; some people seem to handle it well, while others seem to be destroyed. The Holy Spirit will help us not to "burn out" under pressure.

Illustration

Two paper cups are set above a lit candle. One cup does not burn, yet the other one does.

Materials

matches	two candles
two paper cups,	two pieces of window screen
one filled with water	standards to hold the cups

How It Works

A paper cup will not burn when placed over a candle as long as water is in it. When the water is removed, the cup will quickly ignite.

Principle

The water keeps the cup from reaching the kindling point, never getting hot enough to break into flame.

Lesson

We all face pressure in our lives. You have pressure in school to cheat on tests even though it isn't right. You have pressure at home from your parents to get good grades and do what is right. You have pressure from your friends to wear certain things, or to do certain things, or to act certain ways. We all are under pressure.

Some people give in to pressure. They become burned out by it and their will power is destroyed. But others seem to be able to handle the pressures. What makes the difference?

The Lord has promised that if we rely on him he will not let pressure overwhelm us. In 2 Timothy 4:18 Paul writes, "The Lord will rescue me from every evil attack and will bring me safely to his heavenly kingdom" (NIV). Paul is saying that when we come under pressure to do what we know isn't right, the Lord will not let the pressure be too much for us if we trust in him and do what he wants us to do. These two cups represent two people who are being pressured to do something they know isn't right. This one **(show empty cup)** is like the person who is trying to handle the pressure on his own. This one **(show cup filled with water)** is like the person who is a Christian and is letting God help him with the pressure.

(Place both cups over their candles.)

These two cups are under the same kind of outside pressure, but there is a difference in how they react. One is burned while the other one isn't. The same is true for you and me. If we try to handle pressure on our own, we may not be able to, but if we let God handle it and do what he wants, then the pressure won't harm us.

What do you suppose was the difference between these two cups? One had a coolant in it—water. The individual who doesn't give in to outside pressure or burn out under pressure has a certain hidden quality that protects from outside forces. That quality is a relationship with God.

Not only has God promised to help us when we are under pressure, but also James 1:12 in our Bible indicates that we'll be happy if we don't give in and do wrong when we are tempted. For not giving in, we will receive the crown of life that he has promised. God also promises to bless us if we continue to endure under the trials of life.

It is much easier to handle difficult times and challenges if we know that we don't have to carry them ourselves. Because God has promised to help us with these pressures, let him do what he wants to do. However, God does not force us to take his help. He offers it and waits for us to accept. Next time you are facing outside pressure, simply ask God for his help. You'll be surprised how well he answers!

12

The Holy Spirit in Your Life

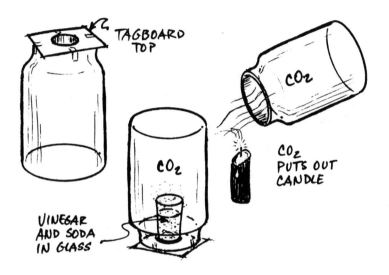

TAGBOARD TOP

CO₂

CO₂ PUTS OUT CANDLE

CO₂

VINEGAR AND SODA IN GLASS

Theme

The fact that the Holy Spirit is in your life is seen by the effect he has, even though you can't see him or feel his presence.

Illustration

A large empty bottle is poured out over a candle and the flame goes out mysteriously, yet it appears that nothing is coming out of the bottle.

Materials

a large glass bottle   a plate
a candle and matches   a glass
baking soda   vinegar in a cup
a piece of tagboard   tape

How It Works

Cut a hole in the center of the tagboard large enough for the glass to pass through. You could tape it to the top of the bottle for ease of handling. Place about a spoonful of baking soda in the glass on the plate so that nothing spills on the table. Have about a half cup of vinegar handy to pour into the glass when the time is right.

As soon as you pour the vinegar into the glass, place the bottle upside down over the glass and allow the mixture to bubble until it subsides somewhat. Then it is ready and the bottle can be gently lifted off and tipped over the candle flame. The CO_2 will flow out and extinguish the flame. You might wish to remove the tagboard from the bottle before you pour the contents.

Principle

The mixture of vinegar and baking soda produces carbon dioxide gas. This gas fills the bottle while it is bubbling. Carbon dioxide is colorless, odorless, and tasteless and is heavier than air. Therefore, as you pour it over the candle, it falls around the flame, shutting off the oxygen supply, and smothers the flame.

Lesson

(Light the candle, placed high enough for all to see. It is the most important element to show.)

What makes Christians different from non-Christians? Answer—Christians have the Holy Spirit in their hearts. In John 14:23 Jesus was talking to his disciples and mentioned that when someone becomes a Christian, he himself would give the Holy Spirit to live in that person's heart.

We will be able to tell that the Holy Spirit is in our lives by the effect that he has on our actions, on our words, and on the things that we think. Paul tells us in Galatians 5:19–21 that acts of a sinful nature are obvious and likely to happen. Some are sexual immorality, impurity, idolatry, hatred, jealousy, fits of rage, selfishness, dissension, and envy. He says, "I warn you, as I did before, that those who live like this will not inherit the kingdom of God" (NIV). In other words, Paul says maybe you're not a Christian at all if you continually live in any of these ways. Your life may be like this bottle, empty, with nothing in it.

(Hold the empty bottle up for the group to see. Then, before placing the large bottle over the glass, put the vinegar into the glass that already has baking soda in it.)

But in verses 22 and 23 he says that "the fruit of the Spirit is love, joy, peace, patience, kindness, goodness, faithfulness, gentleness, and self-control" (NIV). People who have received Jesus will be changed because the Holy Spirit lives in their hearts.

When he came into our hearts, we probably didn't feel anything special. Neither can we feel him or see him now. The Holy Spirit is invisible, but that doesn't mean that he isn't there. That's much like this bottle. There appears to be nothing in it. It must be empty.

(Carefully lift the bottle and pour the contents over the burning candle. The candle will quickly go out.)

However, when I tip this bottle that looks empty over this candle, see what happens? Something in the bottle put out the flame. So, even though we don't see the Holy Spirit, we can see the effect that he has on us. He can help us "put out" some of the bad things we used to do. We won't get mad quite as easily as we once did, we will be able to help others, and we will really want to do what God wants us to do.

13

Our Environment Affects Us

BLOW INTO BOTTLE
TO FORCE EGG OUT

Theme

Sometimes we think that we can associate with the wrong kind of people and they won't affect us. However, generally we get pulled into their activities, which may be doing the wrong things.

Illustration

A hard-boiled egg is pulled into a milk bottle.

Materials

a shelled hard-boiled egg matches
paper or a candle a milk bottle

How It Works

If a hard-boiled egg (barely larger than the opening of the bottle) is placed snugly in the neck of the bottle immediately after placing the fire in the bottle, the egg will be pulled into the bottle. To get the egg out of the bottle, you must tip the bottle upside down and blow past the egg into the bottle. The pressure should force the egg out.

Several reminders are important. First, practice at home before you give your presentation. Second, make sure that your bottle has fresh air in it before lighting the fire. Old, burned-out air tends to stay in the bottle for some time after doing the experiment. You can run some water into the bottle to change the air. Third, be ready to place the egg onto the bottle opening *immediately* after placing the fire into the bottle, as there is not much air in the bottle and the fire will go out soon. You might improve the success of the experiment if you butter the outside of the egg before the experiment, so it will slip into the bottle more quickly.

Principle

When you place something that is burning into a bottle, the oxygen in the bottle is used up and creates a lower pressure inside than outside the bottle. The reverse is true for getting the egg out of the bottle. As you blow into the inverted bottle, you build more pressure inside the bottle than outside. The egg becomes the stopper that holds the pressure inside.

Lesson

How many of you have friends? You can have close friends, and you can have acquaintances. You can have friends whom you have known for a long time, or you can meet a new friend. You can be friends with your brother or sister, and you can have a friend in another town. Friends are people whom we like and people whom we like to be around. Often we become like our friends.

There are two ways to look at friends: those who are good friends and those who are bad friends. The good friends are those who do what is right. They listen to their parents, they tell the truth, and they have a good time with each other. They also will stand with us during hard times.

The bad friends, however, are the ones who don't always do what is right. They may lie on occasion or do things that are not right. We must be strong enough not to be drawn into their influence.

This bottle represents our friends, and this egg represents us. When we associate with these people, we slowly start to get pulled into their group.

(Place the burning paper or candle in the bottle. Immediately position the shelled egg on top of the bottle. It should slowly be pulled down into the bottle.)

We read in 1 Corinthians 15:33, "Do not be deceived; bad company corrupts good morals" (NASB). If we spend time with bad friends, we will become like them, even though we try not to, but if we spend time with good friends, they will help us become better.

If you are associating with some bad friends, then you are like the egg that is stuck in this bottle. How do you get out? The Bible says that if we ask God, he will help us deal with our problems. It may take some time, but he will help us pull out of the group.

(Tip the bottle upside down and blow up into the bottle. This pressure should help to force the egg out.)

14

The Real Difference in People

Theme

It's not the outward appearance that is important; what is in the heart makes the real difference.

Illustration

Two paper bags, hung upside down at each end of a ruler, will remain balanced until you put a candle under one; then that one will begin to rise.

Materials

two large paper bags   a yardstick
a candle   matches
string

How It Works

Balance a yardstick in a string loop. This string can be tied to a pencil that is anchored by a couple of books extending over the edge of the table. Poke two small holes in the bottoms of the two bags and thread two other pieces of string through the holes, tying a knot on the end inside each bag. Hang the two bags on the end of the yardstick by the short strings.

When it is time, place the lit candle under one of the bags, being careful not to get the flame too close to the bag, as it may burn. This bag should begin to rise.

Principle

Air has weight. Heat causes air to expand; therefore it becomes lighter because fewer molecules are in a given amount of space. The bag with the heated air in it will rise as the air expands. If you remove the candle, the rising bag will begin to lower as the air begins to cool.

Lesson

Even though a few things are different about each of us, we are pretty much all alike. We have two arms, two legs, a head, two eyes, a nose, mouth, ears, and a body. As we look on the outside of each other, we see that we look similar to everyone else.

(Hang the bags on the ruler and let them spin around a little.)

These two paper bags represent two people and look quite a bit alike. They are attached to this ruler with some string so we can watch them and compare them. Can you see any differences?

(Light the candle and slide it under one of the bags.)

As we look at people, we see that their hair or eyes are different colors or that they are a little taller or shorter than we are, but we can't see inside other people, or what's in their hearts. Just as with these bags, we can look at the outside and see that they are almost the same, but we can't see what is inside, where the difference really is.

Even though we can't look into a person's heart, God can. God not only sees the outside of a person, but he also looks at the heart, and he says that this is the most important of all. In 1 Samuel 16:7 we read, "The LORD does not look at the things that man looks at. Man looks at the outward appearance, but the LORD looks at the heart" (NIV).

It doesn't matter if we are short or tall, thin or not. The important thing is what we feel in our hearts, how we feel about others, how we treat others, and if we have Jesus in our hearts. If we have asked Jesus to come into our hearts, then people will notice that we show more love toward others. In a sense, we will have a warmer personality, just like the bag with warmer air inside.

We are like these bags; even though they look the same on the outside, it's what is on the inside that makes the difference. We who have Jesus in our hearts won't rise up and float around the room, but people should notice a difference in us.

63

15

Don't Worry About Anything

Theme

Sometimes things that come into our lives cause us to worry. However, we shouldn't worry but should pray and let God take care of them.

Illustration

A plastic ball-point pen cap floats near the top of the water inside a bottle, but when you squeeze the sides of the bottle, the cap will sink to the bottom.

Materials

a large plastic soft-drink bottle   water
two paper clips   ball-point pen cap
wire cutters

How It Works

Nearly fill the plastic bottle with water. Take a ball-point pen cap and make a small hole near the end of the clip part so that a paper clip can be attached to the cap. This can be done with a drill, or you can heat the end of the paper clip over a candle and melt a hole through the clip end. With the paper clip hanging down, drop the cap into the water in the bottle. If the cap sinks, then part of the paper clip must be cut off until the cap stays afloat and upright near the top of the water. If you can't get the cap to sink when you squeeze the bottle after it is tightly capped, then another paper clip must be added. The paper clips are a weight to hold the cap upright. Be sure you screw the bottle cap on tightly.

Principle

The little bit of air in the cap holds it to the top of the water. When you exert pressure around the bottle, the air bubble is compressed into a smaller space and therefore is not able to hold up the weight of the cap. When you relax the pressure, the bubble enlarges again and the cap rises. You can even hold the cap in the middle, if you like, or make it dance.

AV Options

The cap shows up better if you use a clear bottle, not a green one, and shine a light onto the front.

Lesson

(Have the bottle ready at the beginning of the presentation. A volunteer could help with the experiment.)

Most of the time it is fairly easy to stay on top of things in life, just like this ball-point pen cap floating in this bottle. Though there are a few little hassles here and there **(tap the side of the bottle),** we still stay on top of things fairly well. They don't cause us to get discouraged or depressed.

(Ask the helper to squeeze the bottle. The cap will slowly sink to the bottom. When pressure is relaxed, the cap will rise again.)

Generally however, when we start feeling anxious or begin worrying about something, then we are no longer on top of things. We start to sink and feel depressed. We sometimes feel pressure to do certain things. There are pressures to get good grades, to do well in sports, or to dress or act certain ways. Sometimes we are pressured by our friends to do things that we know aren't right. These pressures cause us to worry about what people will think, whether they will like us or not, and about doing something wrong.

God tells us that we shouldn't worry and that we don't have to worry. In Philippians 4:6 we read, "Don't worry about anything; instead, pray about everything; tell God your needs and don't forget to thank him for his answers" (LB). Instead of worrying, all we need to do is turn to God in prayer, asking for his help, and he will help us. The pressure will then be off us, and he will relieve us from our worries. Now, with him taking care of the pressure, we don't have to be down, but we can be on top again.

(Relax the pressure and the cap will rise again.)

16

The Holy Spirit's Help in Understanding the Bible

Theme

Even though the Bible uses simple words that are easy for us to read, we are not always able to understand what it means unless we ask the Holy Spirit to show us what he is saying in it.

Illustration

When you attach two copper wires to a dry cell, hang a paper clip on the end of each wire, and place them about four inches apart in a bowl of water, a light will begin to glow as salt is added to the water.

Materials

a dry cell battery
water
salt
two paper clips
a flashlight bulb and
  socket

three pieces of insulated
  copper wire with ends
  stripped
a large glass bowl
a spoon

How It Works

Attach a wire to each of the terminals of a dry cell battery. One wire should then be attached to one side of the flashlight bulb. The other wire should be attached to a paper clip. With a third wire, attach one end to the other side of the flashlight bulb and the other end to another paper clip. Fill the bowl with clean water. When you put the wires with the paper clips into the water, the bulb will not light up. As you add salt, the light will become brighter. The more you stir in, the brighter it will get.

Principle

This amount of electricity will not flow in clean water until something is added to the water to allow conductivity. The molecules in the salt transfer the current. The more conductive molecules that are included in the water, the easier it is for the power to transfer, therefore the brighter the light.

AV Options

An overhead projector will help the audience see the salt being added and the light becoming brighter. The salt will tend to cloud the water, however.

Lesson

(Place the two wires with paper clips into the glass bowl so they are about four inches apart. The light will not glow.)

Most often when we read the Bible, we can understand what the words are, but sometimes it is hard for us to grasp what it means. Just as in this experiment, we don't see the light. For some reason, we seem to be getting a short circuit; we are not benefiting fully from what we are reading. Therefore, the energy to understand the Bible doesn't reach our minds. Peter, in his second book (1:20), tells us that the Bible is not a group of letters written by men but that it was written by God through men who were moved by the Holy Spirit. In other words, men did not just sit down and write those words in their own power, but the Holy Spirit showed them what they were to write.

(Stir small amounts of salt into the water. The light will become brighter as you add more salt.)

These words, as guided by God, became the books that we have in the Bible. The Holy Spirit used the men to write for him; therefore for us to fully understand what the Bible is saying, we need to ask the Holy Spirit to tell us the meaning of what we are reading.

The Holy Spirit used simple words as he directed the writings. He's not trying to hide the meaning from us, but sometimes we may not understand because we are un-familiar with the the way it is said. It would be like a membership to a secret club for which only you and some friends know the password. To someone else, the word is meaningless and of little use. But to those who know the meaing, it has great value. Similarly, much can be gained from the Bible as long as there is understanding. The Holy Spirit wants to teach us what the Bible says; all we need to do is to ask, and he will help us understand as we read from God's Word.

17

Letting Your Light Shine

Theme

We should not let things that might dim our Christian image affect our lives.

Illustration

The flame of a candle is mysteriously snuffed out when carbon water is poured around its base.

Materials

a clear glass or plastic
   container
a short candle

matches
a bottle of soda water

How It Works

After placing a lit candle in the bottom of a tall glass container, pour some soda water down the side so that the liquid does not touch the flame. The gas from the soda water builds up above the liquid and will soon smother the flame.

Principle

Soda water produces carbon dioxide in the bubbles that fizz up. Because carbon dioxide is the product that results from burning, it is already "burned up" and therefore can not burn or allow combustion. When it settles around a flame, it pushes away the oxygen that is needed to allow a flame to burn.

AV Option

It might be very effective to have the lights dimmed when the candle is lit. The glass container should glow more this way. If you have a TV camera and monitor, it would be excellent to get a closeup of the soda water being poured in and the flame finally being snuffed out.

Lesson

Let's pretend that this candle represents a person. This candle does not have light in it because it represents an unsaved individual. However, when we become Christians, we begin to show some of the goodness of God, almost as if we shine with God's light. As we read in Ephesians 5:8, "For you were formerly darkness, but now you are light in the Lord; walk as children of light" (NASB).

(Light the candle. Hold it up for all to see.)

That Bible verse is telling us that we didn't have God's light before we became Christians, but now that we know Jesus, we have a certain brightness that others can see in us.

(Place the candle in the container.)

In much the same way that this candle brightens this container, we can produce a radiance that seems to shine about us. This light is a pleasant personality, friendliness toward others, a helpful attitude, and behavior that causes others to want to associate with us. Our friends, our families, and the people we are with should see that we have something special, the light of Jesus.

Sometimes, though, we do things that may prevent our light from shining. Sometimes what we say or how we act isn't what God would want us to say or do. On occasion, even our friends might cause us to do something that isn't exactly right. At those times our light might be snuffed out.

(Slowly pour the soda water into the container along the edge, not letting any of the liquid touch the flame. The flame will go out before the liquid reaches the top of the candle.)

You will notice that this liquid will affect the candlelight even before the liquid reaches the flame. Similarly, our radiance will be affected when we do something not expected of a Christian. It's not that we stop being Christians, but others just can't see the light of Jesus in us. No matter how hard we try to let our light shine, we can't overpower the bad things that are evident.

(Try to light the candle. It should be impossible.)

Until we change our ways, we will not be able to have that brightness we had when things were done right. If we want others to see the light of Jesus in us, we must change some of our words or actions and maybe even change some of our friends.

(Pour the water out and relight the candle.)

If we get rid of the bad influence in our life, then we can again radiate with God's brightness in the things we do.

18

Being Aware of Others

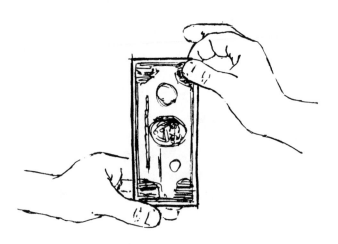

Theme

It is easy for us to know when we ourselves have needs, but we also should concentrate on our friends to know when they have needs.

Illustration

When you drop a dollar bill between your own fingers, it is easy to catch. But when you drop a dollar between someone else's fingers, they won't be able to catch it unless they concentrate.

Material

a flat dollar bill

How It Works

First, hold a dollar bill at one end in one hand. The other hand can be poised with finger and thumb slightly spread apart, just under the bottom end of the bill. When you let go of the bill, the other hand can easily close on the bill as it slips down between the finger and thumb.

Set up the same arrangement with a volunteer, only you hold the bill and the volunteer tries to catch it. Very seldom will the volunteer be able to react fast enough to close the finger and thumb on the bill as it slips between them.

Principle

The mind sends a signal from one hand to the other in an instant. When two people are involved, the catcher must first get an indication that the bill is being released, then send a signal to the fingers to close. The immediacy is lost.

Lesson

Who is the first person on earth to know when you have a need? You, yourself, are, of course! You are able to see a problem or a need and react to it to help yourself. If you have been walking a long way outside and are tired and thirsty and then see a place to get a drink, you head straight over to that place to satisfy your need.

Let me illustrate with this dollar bill how we take care of our own needs. If I hold it in one hand and drop it between my fingers of the other hand, I can catch it fairly easily because I know what is happening. I am sending a signal from one hand to the other and can coordinate a catch fairly easily.

(Drop the dollar bill and catch it a couple times.)

You know, however, that it is not so easy for us to see when others have needs. You and I must be aware of our friends and their needs so that we can help them. We are told in Galatians 6:2 to "bear one another's burdens, and thus fulfill the law of Christ" (NASB). We are to be aware of others in such a way that we can tell when they have hurts or problems, and when they do have a problem, we need to reach out and help them.

Quite often, though, we are so involved with thinking about what we ourselves are doing that we don't pay attention to what is going on in others' lives. As you may remember, it was easy for me to drop this dollar bill and catch it. Who would like to come up and try to catch it when I drop it?

(Let several volunteers try to catch the dollar bill. After they have missed a couple of times, encourage them to concentrate. They might be able to catch it.)

It was much easier for me to catch it than for you, because I was dropping it. You really had to concentrate to catch it because it took a split second for you to pick up a signal that I was dropping the dollar before you could react. The only way you could catch it was to concentrate on my hand. It is not easy to know if our friends have needs, but if we pray and ask God to help us concentrate on them, then we will be able to see their needs and help them. Then we will be able to "bear one another's burdens."

19

Nothing Is Hidden from God's Eyes

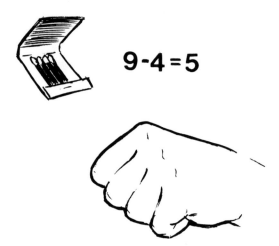

9 - 4 = 5

Theme

Even though we may do things that we think no one else sees, God always sees what we do.

Illustration

You will be able to tell exactly how many matchsticks a person secretly has in a fist by going through a simple routine.

Material

full book of matches

How It Works

Give a volunteer a matchbook and turn your back to that person. Then instruct your helper to follow these three steps carefully.

1. Tear out any number of matches (from 1 to 10) from the book and put them into a pocket or purse.

2. Count the remaining matches silently. Add the two digits of that number together, and tear out that many more matches and put them into a pocket or purse.

3. Tear out any number of the remaining matches in the book and keep them hidden in your fist.

Now you may turn toward the helper, glance at the matchbook, and tell the audience how many matches are hidden in the fist.

Principle

After step 2 is done, there will always be just 9 matches left in the book. Count the number left in the book and subtract it from 9 to reveal the number in the helper's hand.

AV Option

If you can memorize the steps for the process, it will be much more impressive to have your helper blindfold you for the procedure. You can even act as though you are making up the steps of the process, making it appear more accidental and more amazing that you could determine the hidden number at the end.

Lesson

I am going to show you how easy it is for God to know exactly what you are doing, even though you may believe that you are hiding it. I should be able to tell you, without watching, exactly how many matches my helper has hidden in one hand at the end of this procedure. My helper will be selecting the number of matches secretly while following my instructions. I will not know how many matches she or he selects each step of the way.

(Select a helper from the audience. Give the helper a matchbook and go through the routine to determine the hidden number of matches.)

Just because I was able to tell you how many matches you had, don't think that I can see everything. I can see only what I am looking at.

God, on the other hand, is different. He is able to see everything that we do no matter where we are. Whenever we go somewhere, he sees us. We know from Hebrews 4:13 that "nothing in all creation is hidden from God's sight. Everything is uncovered and laid bare before the eyes of him to whom we must give account" (NIV). In other words, wherever we go, God sees us. No matter what we do, we can't hide from him. We will have to answer to him someday for everything we do.

Have you ever caught yourself looking around to see if anyone is watching as you try to snitch a cookie or take something you shouldn't? If nobody is watching, you think it must be all right to take it. If you say something bad or you do something you know you shouldn't do, you may think that nobody sees you. If I can figure out the number of matches being hidden, surely God can do much more than that. I knew the rules for this simple procedure but God knows all the rules for everything. After all, he wrote the rules! It's the same with computer programmers. After they write their programs, they know everything that might happen in those programs. God wrote your program.

We need to look up and realize that even though we can't see God in heaven, he can see us. As the Bible verse taught, there's nothing hidden from his sight. We need to make sure that everything we do is acceptable in God's sight and is pleasing to him.

20

Balancing the Christian Life

Theme

Christians have the responsibility of maintaining a balance in their lives without being extreme one way or the other.

Illustration

A long candle with a wick on each end is balanced on a needle between two glasses. When both ends are lit, the candle will rock up and down striving to maintain a balance.

Materials

a long candle	matches
a long needle	two paper plates
two tumblers (the same size)	

How It Works

Cut away the wax at both ends of the candle so that there is enough wick to light with a match. Push a needle through the candle at the middle and place the ends of the needle on the rims of the two tumblers. Place a paper plate under each end of the candle to catch the drippings.

When the candle is lit on both ends, it tends to teeter back and forth. The candle will seesaw back and forth for hours. When you blow out one end of the candle, the other end will continue to rise.

Principle

As the wax melts more on one end, the candle becomes shorter and lighter on that end and rises, then the other end will melt more, reversing the principle. When you blow one end out, that end will lean down because the flame burns the wax, causing the lit end to become lighter.

AV Options

A spotlight on the candle will cast a shadow on the wall or a screen so the audience can see the action better.

Lesson

Some people think that Christians can't have any fun at all. However, in John 10:10 Jesus said, "I came that they might have life, and might have it abundantly" (NASB). Christians should have a good life and be able to enjoy it.

(Light the candle at both ends.)

Our lives should be as much in balance as possible, much as this candle is. Naturally, we will teeter a little one way or the other as we try to maintain a balance. We are all different and follow our own paths of activities. Some individuals will do a little more of one thing than others, so therefore a balanced life may teeter a little one way at times and totter a little the other way at other times. If we try to keep balanced, we will not lean too much one way by doing too many worldly things or the other way and not have any fun at all.

(Blow out one end of the candle.)

If we don't maintain the balance, then soon we will become unbalanced and will no longer be able to maintain the stable Christian walk that God wanted. We all remember occasions when a friend tried to get us to do something that we knew wasn't right. One might hear, "Go ahead! I've done it; it's great. I didn't get in trouble so you won't either." This coaxing can be very tempting. It's easy to follow someone else's example, especially if they had no problem doing it. Also, we possibly hear that Christians can't have any fun. We might think that we can't do anything but sit at home and be bored.

Fortunately, both of these ideas are wrong. Jesus said that he would bless us if we do what he wants, and part of his blessing is having fun. Good Christians can still have an abundance of enjoyment from life.

21

Being Aware of Satan's Schemes

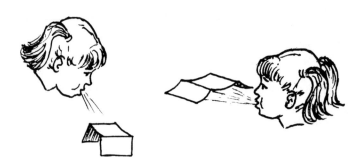

Theme

Satan's schemes are difficult to see, so we must be alert to the different ways he tries to make us fall.

Illustration

A sheet of paper folded into three parts will stand much like an arch. It will not collapse when you blow on its top, but will when you blow through the arch.

Material

a piece of paper (index card weight)

How It Works

A piece of paper 6 or 8 inches long, folded so that the ends will stand down on the table, will create a free-standing arch. The folds should be about a quarter of the way in from the ends.

Principle

Moving air causes lower pressure; therefore, there is more pressure under the arch when you blow down on the top. There is more pressure on the top when you blow under the arch, causing it to collapse.

Lesson

As we look around us, it is easy to count the many things that we can see that have some effect on us. There are also things around us that affect us even though we can't see them. Two examples are the wind and electricity. We know that the wind is there because we see how it messes up our hair. Also, we know electricity is there because the light goes on when we turn a switch.

There is something else we can't see that affects us. Satan tries to bother us and make us fall so we won't do what God wants.

***(Fold a piece of paper into three parts and
set it on the table like an arch.)***

Let's pretend that this piece of paper is a person. It
could be you or it could be me. Satan thinks that his job is
to cause you some trouble. He'll try one way and if that
doesn't work, then he'll try another way. In 1 Peter 5:8 we
read, "Your enemy the devil prowls around like a roaring
lion, looking for someone to devour" (NIV). Satan is not a
real lion, but he tries to scare you as a lion might and
cause you to weaken from some pressure. It might be
when your friends make fun of you. It might be when your
sister or brother breaks one of your favorite toys or a
neighbor calls you names. Satan may use pressure from
outside to try to make you fall.

This folded paper can illustrate an effect similar to
Satan's pressure. You may not collapse from his outside
pressure, such as when I blow down on this arch.

***(Blow gently on the top of the arch. It
should not fall.)***

If acting like a lion and using outside pressure doesn't
work, then he will try something else to get us to weaken.
In 2 Corinthians 11:14 we read that Satan masquerades as
an angel of light. He pretends to be our friend and tells us
what to do, and if he can't trip us up outwardly, then he
tries inwardly. Satan might suggest, "It's not so bad if you
steal just a little." He might imply, "That is not really a lie,
only a little white lie," or urge, "Go ahead and hit him
because he hit you first." Satan is very smart. If pressure
from the outside doesn't work, then he'll try working on
the inside, from the heart. He knows to try many different
things to get us to do wrong. Let's see if our arch will fall
from blowing inside.

(Blow through the arch. The paper should fall.)

If we do fall because of pressure, whether inside or outside, we need to confess to God. He will forgive us and help us get back on our feet again.

22

All Things Are Possible with God

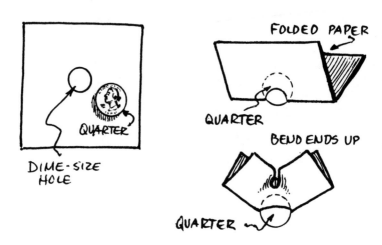

FOLDED PAPER

QUARTER

BEND ENDS UP

QUARTER

DIME-SIZE HOLE

Theme

Sometimes it appears as though our situation is impossible. But if we ask God for help, what seems to be impossible to us may be worked out quite easily by God.

Illustration

A quarter is easily put through a hole in a piece of paper the size of a dime, without tearing the paper.

Materials

a dime   a quarter
scissors   piece of paper
a pencil

How It Works

When you fold a piece of paper so that the fold line goes through the center of the hole, it is possible to bend the ends up, opening the hole enough to let the quarter fall through.

Principle

The edge of the hole becomes straightened as you bend the ends of the paper. Thus, the hole becomes as long as half of the circumference of the hole, which is longer than the width of the quarter.

Lesson

(Ask for two volunteers to help. Give one a dime, the other a quarter.)

I'm going to give each of you a coin and let you keep it if you can do a simple task. Does that sound fair? Hold your coin up for the group to see. Notice that one has a dime and the other has a quarter. The one with a quarter has a more difficult job to do. In order to keep the coin that you have, you must let your coin fall gently through the hole in this piece of paper. The hole in this paper is about the size of a dime.

How many think that the dime can be put through the hole in the paper?

*(Ask the person with the dime to try
gently; the dime should easily fall
through.)*

How many think the quarter will go through the same
hole?

*(Ask the helper with the quarter to see if
the quarter will fall through the hole. Be
careful not to tear the paper.)*

How many think this is impossible? Even though this
looks impossible, it *is* possible, and I know how it can be
accomplished. If any help is needed to put that quarter
through the hole, you need merely to ask for assistance.

*(You will probably need to coax the helper
to ask. Instruct the helper to fold the paper
through the center of the hole. Then, hold
the folded paper on both ends with the fold
along the bottom, and gently place the coin
in the valley of the paper. If the helper
carefully bends the paper upward on both
ends of the valley, the coin will fall through
the hole.)*

Now you have earned your money. This demonstration
is like our spiritual lives. Things may seem impossible at
times, even to Christians, but with God's help, they are
possible. Jesus says in Luke 18:27, "The things which are
impossible with men are possible with God" (KJV).

For example, God tells us that we are to love everyone,
even the boys or girls at school whom you just can't stand
and you don't like even being near. Perhaps they say
wrong things or they put you down, but God tells us that
we must love even them.

So what we need to do is pray and to tell God something like this: "God, this is impossible for me to do on my own, but with you, all things are possible. So I am asking you to help me love that person." It may not happen overnight but God will help you love that person and do what is right.

We may have trouble with many different things, such as doing homework, washing the dishes, or being nice to a brother or sister. For us, it may be impossible, but with God it is not. He is willing to help us; all we need to do is ask.

23

Getting Your Act Together

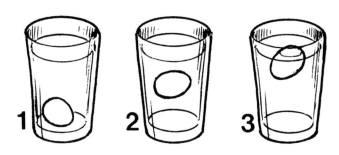

Theme

Your outward appearance is not all that is different from other people. When the Holy Spirit controls a life, changes will occur. Many of these differences, however, are invisible to the eye.

Illustration

Three glasses, each with a liquid inside, will allow an egg to sink to the bottom, go halfway down, or float on the top to illustrate invisible differences.

Materials

three tall drinking glasses   salt
three fresh eggs   rubbing alcohol

How It Works

Fill the first glass with tap water. Be sure to allow enough room in the glass for an egg so it will not run over when the egg is placed in it. Good eggs do not float.

Fill the second glass halfway with water and stir in salt until no more dissolves. You can test the salt solution by placing an egg in it to see if it floats; if necessary, add more salt. Carefully pour the alcohol so it rests on top of the salt water. Tip the glass while pouring the alcohol, or use a ladle.

The third glass will be filled with salt water. Stir in the salt until it does not dissolve any more and an egg will float.

Because the salt clouds the water somewhat, mix enough salt water solution beforehand, let it settle overnight, and use the clearer part of the solution in the experiments.

Principle

Salt adds density to water. The more dense the water, the greater the buoyancy of objects in the solution.

AV Options

For large group presentations, it may be necessary to illuminate the glasses. If you have a desk lamp, lay it on its side under a makeshift shelf of two narrow boards. Separate the two boards so the light will shine up into the glasses that are placed on the boards. The lamp can be hidden with a cloth draped around the front of the shelf.

The glasses can also be placed on the stage of the overhead projector. The light is very bright and can be softened with a piece of tracing paper over the glass of the projector under the drinking glasses.

Lesson

People are different. They look different, they act differently, and they are different inside. Our thoughts, our attitudes, and our emotions vary from one person to another; many of these differences are invisible. These three glasses look almost the same. We forget that the outside doesn't show the main differences. They come from inside. John (7:24) tells us that we are not to judge according to appearance. So let's look inside.

(Carefully place an egg into the first glass containing plain water. The egg should go to the bottom.)

Some individuals are the bottom. They have poor character. Possibly, they are without Jesus. From Romans 8:9 we know that "if any man have not the Spirit of Christ, he is none of his" (KJV).

(Place another egg into the second glass. It should go halfway down, through the alcohol but on top of the salt water.)

Some people have life figured out. They may be getting some help from the Holy Spirit. They are being lifted up, but more work may be needed. In Matthew 26:41 we read, "the spirit indeed is willing, but the flesh is weak" (KJV).

This tells us that some people may want God's help but they are not willing to follow completely what he wants them to do.

(Place another egg into the third glass. The salt water will hold the egg up to the top.)

Some folks are on top of things; they know what life is all about. The Holy Spirit is in the life of such people, and they are following his direction for their lives. We know from Proverbs 14:33 that "wisdom is enshrined in the hearts of men of common sense, but it must shout loudly before fools will hear it" (LB).

The Holy Spirit works in various ways, depending on how people accept his help, but he can make no difference in a person who doesn't accept it. God says in Hebrews 3:10, "I was very angry with them, for their hearts were always looking somewhere else instead of up to me, and they never found the paths I wanted them to follow" (LB).

The more you let the Holy Spirit work in your life, the more it shows, and the better the person you will be.

24

The Purpose of Trials

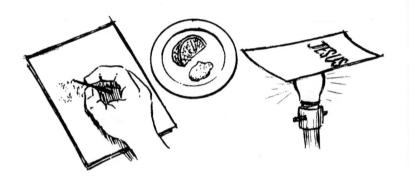

Theme

When we are faced with one of the trials of life, we must realize that God allows it to happen to us so that Jesus will become visible in our lives.

Illustration

The name *Jesus* appears on a blank piece of paper when it is held over a candle or a light bulb.

Materials

a candle   matches
lemon juice   a piece of paper
a toothpick

How It Works

Use juice from a real lemon. Squeeze it out so you can
dip the end of a toothpick into it. Take a piece of paper
and write *Jesus* on it, using the toothpick with the lemon
juice on it. Allow the paper to dry prior to the presentation. The image will become invisible as it dries. Remember where you wrote the word so you can heat that
portion of the paper instead of the entire page.

During the presentation, hold the paper close to the
flame of a candle, being careful not to allow it to burn.
Move the paper back and forth over the heat until the word
shows clearly.

Principle

The heat causes a chemical change to the lemon juice,
turning it brown. In a sense, you are burning the lemon
juice before the paper. The writing will show easily.

AV Options

The heat from a light bulb will bring out the lemon
juice just as well and may be safer. Use a household table
lamp. You can nearly touch the light bulb with the paper
without burning it.

Lesson

How many like to have friends who "bug" you? Perhaps you are being called names or made fun of, or bad things may even be said about you. You don't like it, do you? You don't want these hassles or trials in your life. It would be nice to go through life without problems or bad things happening to us. However, the Bible tells us that God lets these things happen to us for a reason.

(Light the candle. Hold the paper up so they can see that it is blank.)

Let's pretend that this piece of paper represents you or me. If this paper could talk, it would probably say, "I'm having a pretty good time with you today. I enjoy sitting here watching you, and I'm glad that I can be here with you."

On the other hand, if I could ask a question of it, I might ask, "Paper, how would you like to be held over this candle flame?" What do you think it would say? It would probably say, "Oh, no! Please don't put me near that fire! It would be hot, and I might burn!" But, I might have a good reason for doing just that, so I pick up the paper and move it over the flame. I'm not trying to be mean, because I like this paper. I am doing this because I want to show you something special, and you can see it only if I put this paper over some heat.

(Move the paper back and forth across the flame, but do not let it burn.)

Now if this paper could talk, it would say, "Ouch! Oh, this is hot! Please stop!" But I'm not going to stop because I want you to see something special about this blank paper that you can see only if I keep making it hot.

(*Keep moving the paper back and forth until the writing appears.*)

You see, boys and girls, what that something special was? It's Jesus' name! If I hadn't put this paper over the fire and caused it to get hot, then *Jesus* couldn't be seen on the paper.

You know, the same thing is true for you and me. When we have a trial, or when we go through a time that is difficult for us, it is not that God wants to burn us or doesn't love us. God hasn't forgotten about us. God does love us and he wants what is best for us, but he allows us to go through the hard times to allow Jesus to be seen in our lives. In Romans 8:28 we read, "And we know that God causes all things to work together for good to those who love God, to those who are called according to His purpose" (NASB). Therefore we know that nothing happens that he doesn't know about and allow.

But why would God allow these things to happen to you and me? As the next verse says, he allows it so we will become more like his son. Just as this piece of paper had to be put close to the flame and get hot so we could see *Jesus* on it, so you and I need to go through hard times and feel the heat of trials so we will become more like Jesus and so others will see Jesus in us.

25

All Sins Are Equal in God's Eyes

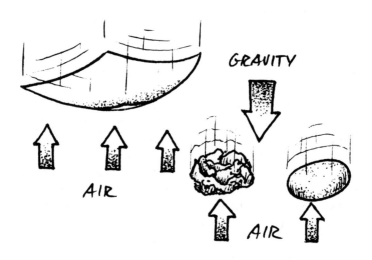

Theme

We often think that certain sins are not as bad as others. Many times we think that a little lie is not as bad as hitting someone. But in God's eyes, a sin is a sin.

Illustration

When a rock and a piece of paper are dropped simultaneously, they will strike the ground at the same time.

Materials

two pieces of paper
a rock that fits in your palm

How It Works

Give the two items to be dropped to the two helpers
and instruct them to drop their items at the same time on
a given signal. You might say, "1-2-3-drop." Ask them to see
if they can tell which lands first each time.

Principle

All objects are pulled to the earth by gravity, no matter
what their weight is. The difference in the way one falls or
floats to the ground is in the design of the object. Some
objects, such as a feather or the flat piece of paper, trap air
under their larger surfaces and create more air pressure
underneath, slowing their falling speed. Surface friction is
also a factor. A larger surface for air to pass by causes more
friction, therefore slowing the object. However, an object
with a smaller or smoother surface has less resistance
and therefore falls more quickly.

AV Options

Ask some of the audience to come up and compare the
weights of different objects so they can tell the rest of
the group. Suggest that they drop the rock and then the
crumpled paper separately. Ask who would vote for the
rock or for the paper, as to which will hit the ground first.
After they have decided which side they are on, drop the
objects simultaneously to show that they fall to the

ground at the same rate. You could use an eraser, a shoe, or some other objects to show that no matter how much they weigh, they still fall at the same rate.

Lesson

(Get two helpers from the audience. Have them hold up two pieces of paper, one flat and the other crumpled into a ball.)

These two pieces of paper weigh the same. One is crumpled and the other is flat. Which will hit the ground first if they are dropped at the same time?

(Drop both of them simultaneously. The crumpled paper will land first.)

Both pieces will fall to the earth at the same rate if they are treated the same. But because we treat them differently, one falls slower than the other, due to more resistance. We do that to our sins also. We treat certain sins differently from others, claiming they aren't as bad as others.

(Now give the crumpled paper to one helper and a rock to the other.)

Now, let's take the winner of the first race and pit it against a heavier and tougher competitor, a rock. If we drop this crumpled paper and this rock at the same time, which of these two objects do you think will land on the ground first, this rock or the crumpled paper?

(Drop both items at the same time. Have the helpers watch closely to see which hits the floor first. Have them tell the audience.)

You see, no matter how heavy the object is, it falls at the same speed as lighter objects because the pull of gravity is the same for both. We may think that some sins are heavier than others. We may think that hitting or beating someone is a worse sin than telling a little lie to our teacher. But we know from 1 John 5:17 that all unrighteousness is sin. In other words, if we sin in doing one thing, it is just as bad as sinning in another way. To God, if we do something wrong, it is equally as bad as something else that we might think is worse. If we lie to our teacher or cheat on a test or take something from a store, it is just as bad as beating up someone or swearing. We need to remember that we might think that one sin is worse than another, but in God's eyes all sins are alike.

We realize that we are punished differently depending on the sin we do. For example, we are punished one way if we kill someone and another if we take something that doesn't belong to us. Yet, each of these actions is a sin, and we need to confess all of our sins to God so he can forgive us.

26

Choosing to Do What Is Right

Theme

Christians should ask God to help with the needs in their lives, but more importantly, they must choose to do what is right.

Illustration

Water will readily pour through a container that has a hole in the top and bottom, until you plug the top opening.

Materials

a container
water
a pan

How It Works

Find a container that can be closed at the top with a cork or a screw-on cap, preferably plastic. Poke a small hole near the bottom on one side. When you fill the container (possibly a plastic beverage bottle), hold your finger over the hole at the bottom, then cap the top and see if any water comes out of the bottom hole after removing your finger. No water should come out, until you remove the cap. A little food coloring in the water is attractive. When you do the experiment, be sure to hold your container over a pan large enough to catch the flowing water.

Principle

When the container is capped, the pressure inside the container remains the same as outside because it is held constant—nothing can come in or go out. The reason nothing can go out is also partly due to the surface tension at the hole, where the outside pressure is pressing against it to hold it in. (You can prove this principle by squeezing the bottle, which will force some of the water out of the hole and leave the bottle indented as you release the pressure. This point has nothing to do with this lesson, however.)

When the top opening is uncovered, gravity pulls the water down and thus sucks air in at the top to maintain equal pressure inside and out. Water is heavier than air, also, so the water goes out the bottom.

Lesson

One of the nice things about growing up is that you get to make a choice about some things. You get to choose which clothes you want to wear. Sometimes you even get to choose what you want to eat for dinner. Having a choice is usually fun, but once in a while having to make a choice isn't as much fun.

When you have a choice to make and you aren't sure what to do, it is good that you can go to God and ask him to give you wisdom to choose what to do, as is promised in chapter 1 of James in the Bible. There are times, however, that you do not lack the wisdom to choose the right, but instead choose to continue doing something that is not right. Suppose that someone says something bad about you or calls you a bad name. Would you be tempted to get mad and call him or her a bad name too? That would be one choice you could make. It is important for you to choose to do what is right, which is what God wants you to do. The right choice would be to turn to God to help control that temper.

In Romans 6:13 we read, "Do not go on presenting the members of your body to sin as instruments of unrighteousness, but present yourself to God . . . and your members as instruments of righteousness to God" (NASB). We need to choose to let God control our lives and follow what he wants us to do.

We will let this container represent you and me. When we lose our tempers, we may also lose whatever respect we may have previously gained. When the bad words flow out of us, we damage our integrity and mar the example we are trying to be.

(Hold container up and let the water flow out of it.)

Now, if we ask God for his help, and choose to do what is right, then he can help us, and our anger or temper or bad words won't come flowing out of us.

(Cover the top opening so the water stops. Release and cover the top opening a couple of times.)

Just as the water stops coming out when I choose to cover this opening, when we choose to let God help us, our temper or bad words won't come out.

27

The Holy Spirit's Convicting of Sin

RUB IN SOME
ASH ON ONE
END OF THE
SUGAR
CUBE

Theme

Even though we show our friends how to receive Jesus, they cannot unless the Holy Spirit is working in them.

Illustration

A sugar cube will not burn when touched by a lit match. But after a little bit of ash is rubbed on it, then it will burn.

Materials

a sugar cube   matches
some ash from a fireplace   metal tongs

How It Works

Holding the sugar cube with the tongs, try to light the cube with a match. You cannot. Next, rub a little ash on one side of the cube. Any ash should work. This time the cube will burn.

Principle

The carbon from the ash becomes a catalyst with the sugar. A *catalyst* is a substance that aids in a chemical reaction but does not itself take part in the reaction. The ash is not combustible and will not change in nature in the reaction. The combination becomes combustible.

Lesson

Christians should witness to their friends. The term *witness* means to tell about something that you have seen or know to be true from experience. To witness for Christ means that we are to tell others about Jesus and how they can become Christians, too. We need to make sure that our words, actions, and character are exemplary so that when we tell others how to become Christians they will listen to us.

Have you ever noticed that sometimes when you tell your friends about Jesus, it seems that they don't even hear what you are saying? They are like this sugar cube here on the table, and you are like this match. You are on fire for Jesus and you are wanting them to catch on fire, too.

(Touch the lit match to the sugar cube a couple of times.)

No matter how many times you try to witness to them, they don't catch the fire of Jesus that you have. You should not stop telling them about Jesus, but there is something else that you need to do. In John 16:8 we read that it is the Holy Spirit's job to convict the world of sin. The Holy Spirit has to be working in people's hearts, convicting of sin, so they will know that they are sinners and need Jesus to forgive their sins.

(Place ash on the sugar cube.)

Now, with both the Spirit's working and your witnessing, your friends may be ready to receive Jesus.

(Touch flame of the match to the ash side of the sugar cube.)

We see then that it is important both to witness and to pray for our friends that the Holy Spirit will be working in their lives. Then they will listen to what we have to say and might receive Jesus as their Savior.

28

Seeing from God's Perspective

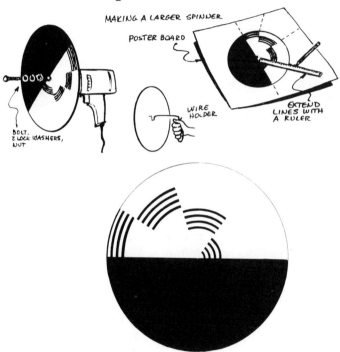

Theme

Many times we view a situation from our own perspective, forgetting that God's perspective may be different. His way is always correct.

Illustration

When part of the group looks at a spinning circle, they see color on the outside and dark circles on the inside, while the others of the group see color on the inside and dark circles on the outside.

Materials

a posterboard circle
an electric drill or bent
   wire
scissors

compass
one round head bolt, two
   washers, one nut
wide black felt pen

How It Works

Cut a circle from a piece of posterboard, as large as you feel will be able to spin on your electric hand drill. Use the felt pen to color the circle as illustrated, using a compass to draw the arcs in each section.

Because the sections are uneven, it might be best to extend the section lines with a ruler from the sample in the back of the book (see the drawing of this process). When finished, cut it out and push the short bolt with a lock washer through the center from the front side. Add another washer and the nut to the end of the bolt and tighten the nut against the back of the board so the bolt will not turn in the board. Put the end of the bolt into the drill and secure it.

Now turn the drill on. A drill that has variable speed control and can be reversed in direction is best. Slow speeds may work best.

A bent wire can be made so you can spin the circle by hand (see the drawing). This technique is also very effective.

Principle

The spinning of this design creates the effect of different colors and shades in the different sections and will reverse the colors and shades when the spinner is reversed. This effect is called "subjective colors."

AV Options

The same phenomenon can be demonstrated over a black and white TV set if you have a TV camera to pick up the picture to allow better viewing from the audience. Color TV may show colors by accident and may not give the pure effect desired.

Lesson

(Show everyone the circle that you are going to spin so they can see the pattern on it. Explain that you are going to divide them into two groups and will show the spinning circle to each group to see if they see any colored lines while it spins.
Spin the circle one way for the first group. Ask what colors they see in the circle as it spins, or if they see any black lines.
Stop spinning the circle and turn to the other group. Spin the circle in the opposite direction. Invite the second group to explain

the order of colors they see from the spinning circle.

Compare what they say to the first group's ideas of the order of the colors seen. It might be interesting to ask each group if the other group is correct or not before telling them that they are both right. Let the whole group see the circle as you spin it again, first one way and then the other. Tell them that they both saw correctly, but that the difference was the way that they saw it. One group saw things one way and the other saw things another way.)

Perspectives can also be different when we have a problem or don't know what to do. When we look at a situation from our own standpoint, we see it one way, just like looking at this circle spinning to the right. Yet when God looks at the same situation, he may see it differently. In Isaiah 55:8–9 God tells us, "For my thoughts are not your thoughts, neither are your ways my ways. . . . For as the heavens are higher than the earth, so are my ways higher than your ways, and my thoughts than your thoughts" (NASB). When we have a problem or need some help we should ask God what he wants us to do, because he sees things from a better perspective than we do.

In Proverbs 3:5–6 we read, "Trust in the Lord with all your heart, and do not lean on your own understanding. In all your ways acknowledge Him, and He will make your path straight" (NASB). We should not try to solve our problems by ourselves, but should talk to God, and he will help us decide what is best to do in any situation.

29

Opposites Do Not Mix

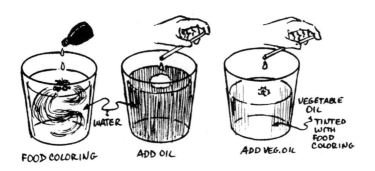

FOOD COLORING   ADD OIL   ADD VEG.OIL

WATER

VEGETABLE OIL

TINTED WITH FOOD COLORING

Theme

Christians are not to be closely tied to unbelievers, and they may feel uncomfortable if they are with unbelievers much of the time.

Illustration

Tinted water added to clear water mixes easily. Stirring oil and water together in a glass will cause them to be mixed for a short time, but after a while they will separate.

Materials

two short drinking glasses   water
cooking oil   food coloring
something to stir with   eye droppers or straws
  (non-wood)

How It Works

Water and oil will not mix. If you stir them together, the oil will break up into small globules at first, but will eventually reunite with the other globules when the stirring stops, forming into a single large globule again. An eye dropper is handy for dropping controlled quantities of oil into the water, or you can use a straw. If you hold your finger over the top opening of the straw, you can carry the amount of oil in the straw to be very effective in your presentation. A release of your finger will allow the oil to run out of the straw when you want it to.

The tinted water is tap water with a couple of drops of liquid food coloring added.

Use a nonporous item for stirring so the oil does not soak into it.

AV Options

If you use a petri dish (different sizes are available from your neighborhood school), you should be able to project the tinted water and the oil onto a screen for larger audiences. Place the petri dish on the glass stage of an overhead projector; the light will project through everything. A clear plastic pie cover (from a graham cracker crust sold in the local grocery store) may also work on the overhead.

Lesson

We know that when we become Christians, Jesus takes away all our sin and changes our lives. Before we became Christians, however, we probably spent a lot of time around other non-Christians and enjoyed doing what they liked to do and saying the things they said.

(Put a partially filled glass of water on the table.)

The water in this glass represents someone who is not a Christian. Other non-Christians are able to associate with this person without much difference being seen or felt.

(Pour a little tinted water into the glass and stir.)

See how easy it is to mix with the old group? But, just as this water seems to be slightly tinted, they may be doing things that are a little questionable, maybe not entirely good.

(Put a few drops of oil into the water.)

If a person becomes a Christian, being with non-Christians may not be as much fun because they have different values. A Christian is a new person with new interests, represented by this oil. In 2 Corinthians 5:17 we read, "Therefore, if any man be in Christ, he is a new creature; old things have passed away; behold all things are become new" (KJV). When we become Christians, our bodies are still the same, but we become different inside. Therefore, we like different things, we'll act differently, and we are not like we were before. We may not enjoy doing all the things we used to do with our old friends. If we realize that the old friends are involved in questionable activities sometimes, it might not be as much fun being with them as it once was. Even though we may still have some fun with them from time to time, down in our hearts we know that we shouldn't mix with them as we did before.

(Stir the oil and water so they mix as much as possible.)

Notice how the oil doesn't seem to mix with the water, just as it should be with us. As time goes on, we simply won't feel a part of the old group any more. We don't want to stop being friends with them, but we will not enjoy the same things any more. We will probably start to find friends with similar interests who want to follow God's desires.

(Pour oil into a glass with oil in it.)

From reading the Bible we know that we are not to stop being friends with non-Christians, but that we also need to find others whom we can be closer to—ones who want to do what God wants.

30

Controlling Our Tempers

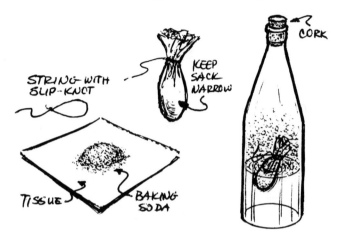

Theme

You are all aware of someone who has a temper, either yourself or someone else. Everyone should know how to control their temper and how to help someone else learn control, also.

Illustration

A bottle filled with a vinegar and water solution will blow its cork off when a baking-soda-filled napkin comes in contact with the solution.

Materials

a soft-drink bottle

a thin napkin or toilet
tissue

baking soda

vinegar water

a string

a cork

How It Works

Mix enough equal parts of vinegar and water to fill ¼ to ½ of the bottle. Put about a teaspoon of baking soda into a thin napkin or a piece of toilet tissue and tie it together with the string. Be sure the tied napkin is not too thick to go into the bottle neck. The cork should be able to fit tightly into the bottle top when needed. Drop the napkin into the solution at the right time, then cork the top tightly and make sure the top is aimed where no damage can happen from the speeding cork when it pops. The cork will hit a high ceiling in a convention center (just to give you an idea of the force).

Principle

When the solution wets the baking soda in the napkin, carbon dioxide gas is formed. This expansion of substance in the bottle creates more pressure inside than outside, causing the top to blow off.

Lesson

(The partially full bottle of vinegar and water solution should be ready. Have the cork handy and the baking soda tied in the napkin.)

Does anyone know a person who has a bad temper? Maybe you yourself or someone else does. You never know when that person will explode.

(Put the napkin with the baking soda into the bottle and cork the top tightly. Be sure to point the bottle up and away from anything fragile, because the cork blows vigorously. You may have to tip the bottle to get the napkin well saturated. Do not point it at anyone!)

The Bible indicates that *having* a temper is not wrong, but that *losing* a temper is wrong. In Proverbs 19:19 we read, "A man of great anger shall bear the penalty" (NASB). In other words, when you don't control your temper, you will have to suffer the results of losing your temper. For example, if you get mad and hit something, then you will have to live with a sore or broken hand for a while. If you get mad and yell at someone, you may have to live with the fact that you have lost your friend for a while. Or, if you lose your temper and break something, you will have to live with a guilty conscience for breaking it, or you may have to buy another one if it belonged to someone else. Furthermore, you may also be punished for losing your temper.

Our friends don't know what is going to make us lose our temper, just as we didn't know when this bottle was going to blow open. So, if we get mad and blow up, we may lose some friends.

If we have a problem with a temper, we need to ask God to help us control it. And when we realize that we are getting mad and are about to lose our temper, we need to stop right then and pray to God for help. And if we do lose our temper, we should confess that sin to God. He has promised to forgive the sins we confess.

If you have brothers, sisters, or friends who have problems controlling their tempers, you need to help them, too. From Proverbs 15:1 we learn, "A gentle answer turns away wrath, but a harsh word stirs up anger" (NIV). This proverb suggests that we not make fun or deliberately say things to get them mad, but say things to help them stay calm and control their emotions.